Bruises
adam Shove

Bruises
Copyright © 2023 adam Shove
DARK THIRTY POETRY PUBLISHING
ISBN: 978-1-7392546-8-1

Shove, adam
First edition

Artwork by Jessica Ellison
DTPP14

Books by adam Shove

I Feel So Bad, I Thought You'd Want To Know 2011
Lucid 2015
Laconic 2016
Postcards To Dogmatic Voices 2017
...and The Past Was Now 2017
Last Night And This Morning 2018
The Vodka Diaries 2019
Coast 2020
Photogenic Afterthoughts 2020
Fling 2021
Desire 2022
Bruises 2023

DARK
THIRTY
POETRY
PUBLISHING

For my barber Chey, thank you for the wisdom.

Lake Shore Drive

Eyes to the skies,
Live and hardcore,
Buffalo fresh;
Back to the thrift store.
Lazy eye shown,
Not quite David Koresh.
Laughed out shotgun blown,
Forget my name,
Guyville won't ever change.
But a change is gonna come,
Sam Cooke said
Both before and after corruption happens.
City state of mind.
Recognise the badge?
Chicago Black Sox.
My schematics sound Def Jux,
This look rang out Dischord.
Even when I was homeless,
My words went into export.
Nothing came at length I'm not Cervantes,
The next line was cryptocurrency,
Don't mess with me,
Perkovich is my fraternity.
Blacklight and key lime pie,
Sleight of hand with a baseball stance.

Wacker Drive

Who else acknowledged that poetry is dead,
Guess we're all zombies.
Knowing I'm eastern,
How was it you all referred to me,
Commie?
Faux anonymous
Should have been lost with the cistern,
Monotonous refrain
In the pages of multiple books,
Would you rather I acted 96 Common
Or 2005,
Be it Stakes Is High,
You can't fall off
If you never fell on.
We both know there was truth
In you plagiarising,
I can spell it both forwards and backwards,
Everyone knows your name's not Jacquelyn Lee
It's revealing.
All the while six words on a page,
So let me rebuild,
Before the next line is set to engage.
Stuck copying others,
Back must be ripped
From being caught on deadweights
Or barbed wire,
Duck next time
You wouldn't want to get hit with skill.
Chardonnay and still eating beef,
Nothing more than cash cow
Unsure how to leave.

Pulaski Park Featuring Kindra M. Austin

Jessica gave me a reminder,
In a world full of pasta
Don't be spaghetti.
Find a vodka that with absinthe sugar,
Cooks up sweeter.
I stay here pushing on for better things
So we're not empty,
These are the starts of the better days,
Out the park in this home run.
Here the poets secrets
Were passed about like opiates,
Now we're realists,
Feminists still hoping on change
Looking over the future
Forgetting our associates.
Then I heard carnivores
Had been trying to speak up,
You want to fuck with my sister
I'd put the poets sword between your eyes,
The boring parts would flash
In less than a fraction of time.
If I had put the original of the next line
You would have wished you were blind.
This is the first time today
I'm going to pass the pen.
I knelt 'neath deaf stars, empty of wishes
And full of bitches 'bout unprecocious poets.
Sister says that I'm a snob cuz I don't bob
On instadick. Don't worry Sis, I get my prick,
But poet prostitution?
Nah, leave that shit too Plain and Simple.

Have you seen me? I'm a gothic symbol.

Forest Glen

I see poets think they're hot
But then sugar crash
On Girl Scout cookies,
The oscillation of heat or AC
As the weather can't decide when it wants to be,
What it truly wants
In October, April or July.
What was it they were telling me
I was shallow,
But my metaphors had more depth
Than the cheese in your pizza.
Caught between
The Argentina short ribs,
H. H. Homes murder castle that burnt down crib.
Remnants of fishscales
Didn't happen between us,
This city becomes dark too much
Reminding me of the 23 on the Bulls jersey.
Cyberpunk are you game at all?
I see right through,
Don't let the dust settle in the jazz club,
Horn section,
Play out,
Play on play on.

Marynook

Words that have been falling down the stairwell,
Continuous layers of graffiti blank canvas
Covering up the previous bombshell.
Next thing that I steal will be a tattooist,
you know Norman Fucking Rockwell.
The bruises that we each endure
Shouldn't be semicolons
Or instructions to this catalyst.
I wasn't sober enough to remember
The reason as to what made me go vegetarian,
Popcorn and much more
Before you realise the movie of life
Is closer to the end credits.
No second takes or edits,
I wish I had
Jacquelyn here
To feel free to rant on the engine
To being a vegan.
Guess she doesn't write anymore.

South Sangamon Street Featuring Rheign

Alligator hoodie,
Range of a calculator
That explains logarithms,
Numbers I'd understand
Or hardly.
I ripped up classical silences,
Iambic pentameter,
Break-loops from the DJ
Who was told he'd be nothing more
Than a janitor.
Time falls into reverse of the absences,
Trying to decide
Between nunchucks and throwing stars,
Spell out every answer from lancer picks,
Pistol-grip before the brawl
Gets to the bar.
Duck quills
While each guest
Doesn't let their wordy ideas slip.
Copulating couples confiscating crumbles,
Now it's time to pass the pen yet again.
Doormen and barred windows
Lone trees and brick slabs,
— Ideologies that fight —
Grass patches and taxi cabs.
People just hustling, bustling in sight
Blaring bass in their eardrums,
Glory and gore win the fight
Ignoring the sirens around them;
Strolling South Sangamon Street
Night and day
With the mindset of the masses

Stoic so they look brave.
Headlines and doom scrolling
— The zeitgeists —
We treat them as the holy, the Righteous
And our weapons to fight back with:
Silence or violence.
Bullets to bullet point pens
We have a choice,
An issue we can no longer avoid
Held by invisible chains;
We need to protest the way we behave,
And we can make a change
If we take it day by day.

Wrigleyville

So many people try to explain
How this city is like a paradise lost,
An immaculate perception
That got paused,
The loop might not be fully affected
By the thaw.
But is it going emphasise gloss.
When all that was left was you
And that disavowed victory in hopscotch,
Trying to justify
When your voice is burning up from troche.
Chinatown touchdown scream,
I started this with no theme,
The day takes itself apart.
While I'm lost
Wandering with a shopping mall kart.
Graffiti punchline
Broom swept away the asinine,
John Coltrane beats
Reverberating in alkaline.
Tomb starts in the womb,
Skeleton blacked out mouth Mendelssohn.
Cubs and Bears,
Opposite sides of the city;
But always come as pairs.
Incognito apsara,
Though this poetry packs the punches,
Cassius taught me
Only the best get to be judges.
Southpaw to an orthodox stance,
Glance for a moment
Before aiming for the jaw.

East Beverly

I ask so many questions,
My suggestion
Is if you want me to behave
Don't lay out all the weapons
In front of me.
Hostile at the dinner table,
Overdose on syrup or maple.
Glucose found in these pancake shoes,
Wrapped up tight with milkshake blues.
I tried to explain
That writing isn't the end to a means,
I have to work every hour of the day
Otherwise I'd have holes filling up
All my goddamn jeans.
Who told you it was fashion,
There's only one action
Which is the fraying on the seams.
All I ever seem to do is disagree,
So shut your fucking mouth;
Eat your processed meats
With cannellini beans.

Bridgeport Featuring Beth Voetsek

I wouldn't murder the sheriff,
But if he double crossed me
With the pen,
You'd never call me the plaintiff.
I wouldn't want to invite poets
That would make me think
That I'm dividing the classes,
Even with a megaphone
This isn't music for the masses.
Set up the funk notes and watch
As the words pour before I rip,
Next thing to happen is a scissor kick.
I'm ready to go ZOSO are you?
The lights show blue at night.
Raise it an octave
Before I pass the pen.
BITCHES LIKE BOYS,
WOMEN CREAM OVER CARS AND MONEY,
I AIN'T INTERESTED
IN JUST ANYONE'S CHUTNEY.
COME TRY IMPRESS ME
WHEN YOU ROLL IN
WITH A MATTE BLACK 720 S,
YOU DON'T KNOW THE MANUFACTURER,
GUESS.
I WANT SUICIDE DOORS
SO I GET IT WHEN YOU DON'T LOOK.
WOULD YOU LISTEN TO THE WORDS I SPIT
IF I DIDN'T EXPOSE MY ASS AND TITTIES,
YOU WANT MY SKIRT SO SHORT
YOU MISTAKE THIS DECADE
WITH THE MINISKIRTS IN THE FUCKING SIXTIES.

Am I suppose to believe
You caught chlamydia from a toilet seat?
Pizza?
That blonde bitch
You said got your dick hard like Khaleesi.
Hey adam,
Thank you for the space to place my thoughts.
I wish I had a voice like Neneh or Mabel.
I don't have a home,
Don't try and call me,
You'll just be ignored.
Life with this bitch contains no reward.
Just ask adam.

Humboldt Park

Whereas these days
It's all snot samples and quarantine.
And now we find conjecture
Based dyslexic poets
Who don't wish to be anything more
Than a philistine.
Anxiety won't save a spot at the table,
Tattoo onto the reparations cheque
Dissolve into the abstract of these fables.
The shoestring that I work on
Doesn't leave me with anything
To give the bill collector,
Cabin fever budget
With the world
As it continues to rot in multiple sectors.
Back to the dyslexic,
I mean I know I'm eccentric
You however consider yourself arithmetic.
I can see how your brain
Is more empty than Houdini's grave,
Engrave your name
With the same letters as the Bears,
Or would you rather the lizard people?
Don't forget we're all equal.

South Lawndale

Arpeggiate the sequence
Reversing it back to its inception,
Slang words found on graffiti
Next to the overpriced skyscrapers reception.
Metro day passes
Smoked away
As they still expect double on our taxes,
Who forgot to say
This is the purple book,
I don't hand out compliments,
I fire shots
And leave everyone shook.
There was a reason behind
A lack of table of contents,
It would only yell FIRE.
Radioactive,
What reading are you getting on your Geiger?
Oh how you should have spent more time
On your poetry,
Guess not all of us
Could afford topiary.

Jackowo

Exhale the fumes and pheromones,
The city lacks catacombs,
Demolished buildings whereas city hall
Still has the blueprints.
Weak links falling apart as my words
Tesselate tether,
Total trigger tinker tailor tied together.
Snapdragon petals resemble skulls in death,
Which doesn't matter any more or less
Than life;
I couldn't count fully to your debt.
The macabre ideas
That nature offers,
Even with the snow it's a high degree.
I watch the type casting,
Somebody out there gives zero shits
When they proceed their spending spree.
Ride as I find myself
Hypnotised by you.
It's all philosophical
In the colours of bruises.
We ain't getting out of this alive,
It seems like to me
That these streets
Have the chaos
Of the contents of a beehive.

Old Town Triangle

I try to avoid having topics get political,
But can someone explain the truth
With Peng Shuai?
A counterbalance
Before it all looks mysterious and satirical.
I guess it's a detox,
You think I understand ewoks,
And feng shui.
Tomorrow shouldn't be foreseen,
Nothing can truly be considered a promise.
You can say stay safe,
Words wont help uncover the darkness,
Untethered in paradigms.
The bleakness of the city limits
Makes me want to don a parka,
Speaking words of Kafka.
Who am I kidding,
Can we venture out to the hitting,
Pretending we're each Naomi Osaka?
Interrobang setup the words that you know,
Do you really want me to hit a Nas flow?
Wishing that it was all remedial power,
You'll never see Eloy Jiménez
Drunk on vodka.

Avondale

The price of our ignorance
Will be extinction,
There's nothing hidden within this cipher,
No words lost to this encryption.
A bittersweet dissonance,
A fraction of microchopping thoughts,
Births ideas
That should have been omnipotence.
Life fluctuated
While I had no clue
On how to sample in poetry,
It was ok I worked without depth;
Emotionally
Though still brimming with diplomacy.
Baby, fall back by the next time
I scratched baby out of the pages
In the barrages of maybe;
I don't fully understand
Guess I'm crazy.
When people wanted to consider themselves
To be dangerous,
It was a misconception,
An introspective way
Where detail is in the attention.
Was my momma right,
It's the wrong era to be alive in poetry?
Does she mean
Words have lost their potency?
Guess it's true,
Depending on your geolocation;
The revolution is unwilling
Yet again it could be unable
To be televised.

North Sheridan Road

I was grateful
For the dead and closed answers
That I could give,
Waiting on the room to pick up its volume
Allowing me to relocate them all
To Sheridan or Wicker.
I was often drunk as the images accommodate
In my memory picture,
What little do I know,
I went on a date with a trans woman
And I'm the only one
Who didn't seem to be bothered.
Nothing was said or done to be ironic,
At times it was almost feeling myopic,
Though if I hadn't kissed her
I'd call it a moment squandered.
I'll simmer my thoughts down,
I wouldn't fire a shot at her just yet,
I guess in hindsight
She was only a gold digger.
Should have told her,
All my fillings fell out.
I've never claimed to have the answers,
It's the purple sugar coated prophetic
That fall into place.
And where were you?
Righteous poet,
Where were you?
Perfect teeth,
Still a hypochondriac missing
The improvisations in my conscious stream
Without a beat.
I know you tried to mention my effeminate walk,

That's the results of years being fearless,
No helmet style Tony Hawks.
The only bad night's sleep I get
Is from my dystopian government.
I can't believe that a shrink once recommended
I eat meat and take supplements,
When the truth was found
In hickory smoked tofu, avocados, spinach
And the mercy given to both knowledge and land.
Seriously where are you?

Dunning

Her name wasn't one
I could remember,
Still she craved a satyriasis,
It wasn't even
To be a sex fiend by nature.
Put your feet up
As we loop through the purple line,
We'll get drunk on expensive wine,
Passing it through a brown paper bag.
I couldn't retrieve my thought
From the original,
Chances are it could have been wack.
A protest
Burning a president effigy,
Still we'll be alright.
A house full of millionaires
Don't comprehend the totem or stairs
Of austerity.
Where should we get off?
Are the cubs in game mode tonight?
Should we try to sneak on top
Of the outer buildings?
There was a reason for the twentieth century,
Recorded sounds and the cholera epidemics,
While the rest became a documentary.
I guess everything else
Could have been left as an appendix.

Sleepy Hollow

We smuggle on the east side,
Heading south;
Why do you use Google Maps for a guide?
We're running down deep,
Going to make trouble the bitch now.
Dismantle the shotgun,
You said it was done quicker
Than you could say somewhere or somehow.
White van jumping red lights
And that spells trouble,
A Rolex Daytona on your wrist
Not that you try to stay humble.
This was starting to feel different,
Remember the first time
You heard Kanye West samples?
I got nothing to lose but the blues,
Even though what I was after was purple.
Slowed down
It started to act way too close to The Matrix,
Flowed before it parted in a fight scene,
Moses wasn't the only to employ theatrics.
One, two, three,
It's kind of dangerous in poetry,
Liars steal your words
Regardless of your country.
I blurbed a book into a thesis,
Now all I ever say is
Good Jesus.

Norwood Park East

New revolution it all falls into place
Like a bipolar,
Dressed up and I can still see the bruises
On your shoulder,
Change me, change you
Wile E. Coyote is immortal
Ask the boulder.
My memories recollect
On the west and east coast seashores,
Though I'm not seeing either
From this perspective,
Everything falls into place
Whether it's understood in retrospective
Or not
I'll explain when I exit the door.
Did it matter
That it was all the words
Of this collective?
Recycled ideas were in full effect
When lockdown happened,
My outfits underrated that's the problem,
Look what I did with the purpose
Of a misunderstood culture.
I neither consider this harden, or soften.
Diplomatic was forgotten,
Derelict buildings
Never have the right to stand.
I couldn't write with my left,
So I use my other hand.
Last time I mentioned 33
The city said Kareem,
Now they love Pippin.
Presidents fortunately are temporary,

Wu-Tang and musing on Kenzie Harr are forever;
That woman's the vixen.
All the same,
I was considered to be a lexicon junkie,
Faded T-shirt 1977 continuous tour
Led Zeppelin.
Four nights ten years prior to Scottie.
I fulfilled the actions I said I would,
They were in an order
So nonlinear,
My feelings went deep,
And my thoughts were deeper.
I didn't know
If it could have really been the grim reaper.
I know that you should
Respect my thoughts.

LeClaire Courts

A prohibition Robin Hood
Orchestrated
The Saint Valentine's Day massacre,
Guess that was the blueprints
For Chi-Raq,
Doesn't matter about the day on the calendar.
Duckworth got out
As we both know there's no reward
In the heavens of violence,
How much would you find in the rivers?
Cold case evidence.
While I'm not recognised here,
I reckon that's a good thing.
A stranger doesn't smile,
Just looks ahead,
Hearing snippets of the murmurs said around.
What I overheard in Chicago,
Do you speak for the masses
Or just drill hall aficionado?
The weather will fluctuate
Beyond all I can explain
Within the legato.
Now I find myself trapped in a retrograde,
Loose but I should have known,
I should have known,
Nobody would hesitate
In how nothing was seen
In front of the magistrate.
Arcade games and other irrelevant aspects
To my life,
Spades and cars falling asleep
With dream-walking
That appears contrived.

Gage Park Featuring Joel Anthony Ciaccio

I can write a right,
Don't mistake me for a perfectionist
I'd never try to hide a mistake
Or rewrite a wrong.
My words don't expect me to protect,
Wise men don't talk
Just for the sake of it,
The silence never muttered by philosophers
Respected or headstrong.
Before you sink another drink,
With words not wisdom
And admit between blinks
The lies you tell your shrink.
Poets that I asked to be guests,
The ones who rejected me
Wearing Dennis Rodman numbers on their chest.
The arbiters
Who pick wrong at every point in life,
I pray that you survive
At more than your mind.
Somebody else knew what I meant
In my house of leaves,
I'll pass the pen
And see just what it achieves.
Many things come to mind now:
Your leaves, they left the page long before
You could lock your hardcover house
Tight, like a teen's high school journal.
A tree in autumn that holds its water for later,
The bound reams of paper to make up
Her sparse shadow never shows how many rings she has inside.
The rest she hides, keeps hidden under

Her mattress. The record of her day is pressed
By the book of her heavy head
Every night, thinks: I'll sleep when I'm dead.
But her writing never reads, only has time
To transcribe dreams in the ink of thought
For fans who subscribe.
That's blacker than Dennis Rodman with no jersey on.
What is the number of her darkness? "The hustle"
They say is what pays the bills,
But "by the book" also means, strictly adhering to the rules:
The invisible prison bars of the perfect. Poor girl.

Arcadia Terrace Featuring Christina Hennemann

Waiting in the silence of the ideas
Just to let them breathe,
I only require a minute,
You understand Julianna Peña,
And those she put beneath.
Should we get front row tickets?
An idea that comes out
Of the purples and whites,
Saturday night fights.
When they said
That the words needed to be in the pocket,
I looked beyond the tower
And included the picture
Across the camera sprockets,
Theatrics placed inner peace helix,
I swear often but now you hear
The drunken toddler trinkets.
Gabriela Dawson couldn't put out
The words I had written,
Shame I can't pass any of this
Through a distortion pedal.
Harwood Heights along with the truth
In what was happening
Within those macabre ideas
That were the after effects
In ice hockey circles,
Grey Poupon
Layered before we went all collapsed neutron.
I need to read,
Watch as I pass the pen
Before it all gets shred.

I swallow ink and steal his pen,
let my feet print the simmering tar
In the fiery July heat.
How I missed the burning sun
In my rainy refuge.
My fingers trace the broken terracotta,
Dusty pillars,
Where Adonis once seduced an innocent Venus,
And I draw history into the pen.
Safely stored,
I carry the scenes to the sea,
Hoping those memories that are not my own
Will sink into the Greek papyrus,
Effortlessly perhaps.
The moths wrap their wings around me at night,
Spinning thick grey hairs,
But in the sand,
Waves splashing softly before me,
My chest opens and the ink flows out.
He always told me to relax,
His seaweed hair and
Salty upper lip tickling my ocean.
His words are writing ancient love poems anew,
His pen in my hand,
His stories now led by my mouth,
My magpie-fingers.
I am not really writing about him,
Though, as he is not a Greek Adonis,
And I am not his Venus.
I don't have a shell to crawl back into,
Clams closing so he'd never find his pen again.

Edison Park

The lack of curvature that exists
On the city streets
Didn't take place
When looking at you
In your tight light blue jeans,
My residence is on the verge of poverty,
Though the knowledge of man
Couldn't be quantified.
Asking for the number nine or fifteen,
The blank look wasn't happening in between.
If the day is progressing slowly,
Do you think it's worth going to find a katana?
Pawn shop finds,
When what I really want is a retro car,
Low rider,
Black with purple on an E30.
The life of a widow or divorcee,
I can only speak from the point of view of one.
I admit that both me
And the universe have strange powers,
Look up and wait for the heavens to open up;
When will we have day showers?
Meanwhile the only thing I learnt this week
Is that both my employers
Don't know how to listen,
That was already on my cards,
Would I call it a prediction?
No.
The Willis Tower rising above it all,
Roger Brown just seemed to look at it
From a parallax.
My brain falls back to reality,
And I smell the lilacs.

Gresham Featuring Faye Alexandra Rose

While the words didn't resonate with me
I guess I don't spend enough time
In the 312, it's all 773,
On the south side,
Richard Dent MVP
That you couldn't conjugate me.
A didactic response
That should have been psychoanalysed.
Hear this my co-sign was so much more
Than eye candy,
Intricate geometric wordsmith
As the hanging baskets blossom
In the September barometric.
An ellipsis in the metaphors
Which defy the definition
Of our social structure,
It might be August or October,
Season's happening
For the dopest of thunder.
Blind season is almost upon us,
Can anyone translate Lollapolloza?
Western world when we're done with this,
Should we retire and move to Nova Scotia?
The benefits of a poet
Who knows how to switch off and dream,
does such a thing exist?
These bones are our home
And we are cursed with the pain
Of remembering.
The hungry wolf hunts faster,
Snarled lips, grief sinks it's teeth.

A poet is not whole without pain
- Words upon the page -
Beg to unravel,
For a softer world,
Grace upon our skin.
We suffocate in nuance,
It traps its victim with melodies of imagery
And metaphors with false enticement.
Instead it shreds our soul
To reveal what we knew to be true
All along.
But we dream our words can change the world,
We dream our words can change one world,
We dream in spite of the pain,
We dream because of the pain.

Douglas Park

It's all soul poetry
That wasn't in this quadrant,
Blank notes
Written on erasable parchment,
While the insomnia continues
From our dystopian government.
Observing the falling from digrazia,
Nights twitch in and out
Of which it was all designed
As mass hysteria.
West side attitude
The women remind me of my muse,
How could I compare anyone to Kenzie Harr?
And there's something in my spirit,
It tells me
There's so much beauty in the city
And I guess I saw it more today.
All we have is time,
And this could be when your teeth
Were resting into my nerve,
An understanding of how we could co-exist
When all I am is a herb, I vore
The words that take me to places
South of this cities Westchester,
Zealous fashion design,
Is that more important
Than the secrets which I tell my hairdresser.

Fulton River District Featuring Beth Voetsek

Not much happens,
Especially as I'm an antisocial pessimist,
Is there need to have hooks,
Ear worms that grow forming dragons.
Entering the dragon,
Shaolin style fever dreams
And sleep paralysis detected in books.
Can I reread Sun Tzu?
Watermark trepidation in the picture frame,
And the foliage looks right
Even if it leaves me confused,
Oh can I scream!
Remember Refused.
Knowing that I saw
What was taking place behind
The anxious cigarette smoke,
The lime wedge in the bottom of the glass,
Like that night in Park Mesa Heights.
My bank account perpetually reads broke.
Beth it's all happening within these pages,
I don't remember that parable.
Remind me please.
HONESTLY I CAN'T REMEMBER,
THERE'S SO MUCH GOING ON.
AND WHILE THE WHOLE WORLD
WAS CAPTIVATED BY THE CASE
OF DEPP VS HEARD,
NOBODY CARED ABOUT THE IMPENDING DOOM
I HAD.
I THINK I SHOULD BE SEDATED,
THAT'S THE WORD.
DO YOU READ ME?

Am I slept on?
Should I have a cigar
And a car that's my own?
Not one that's stolen.
All I want is an abortion
To the patriarchal transponder.
We could be outgunned,
But never lose a manhunt.
I feel the need to remind you
How you watch when nothing is happening,
Don't listen
As the truth won't be found.
Guess I will see you in the hotel
After the cities.

Chrysler Village Featuring Rheign

Burning rubber like we were heretics,
Control in a stolen Lexus,
Give me a manual,
And we can race up from Texas.
Wild nights
As we race towards
The solar rising plexus,
The next race we have
The rule is simple,
No modifications,
And if the law say
Our speed makes us criminal,
Say nothing.
They might try and chop your words up
Like a J Dilla record.
As I'm not in Europe,
I'd take
A blacked out Buick Grand National.
Baby what would you pick
As your ride?
with you by my side
that's the greatest of all time.
vintage Mercedes ride,
that's the cool cat kind.
sunshine lighting our way,
feeling the blue breeze
lined with dying citrus trees swaying
forget about someday
we're going today.
we see we conquer
we'll dance anyway.
wishing we could change

what we said,
leaving our regrets in the sand.
setting ourselves apart on the stand,
shifting gears and rock n roll bands
you Stan, no conversations
just focused on new temptations.
burning rubber in friendly places
having fun and entering a new phase -
a highway headspace.
Maybe the only way
We can truly enjoy these
Chicago street tracks,
Is when we live as copilots
While being insomniacs.
Whereas if anyone says
We're driving too fast
And we see blue and white lights,
Though the sirens sound
So much more apt
When we're doing this at night.

The Loop

But I didn't hear a thing
When you played your Telecaster,
The frequency wasn't there
Regardless of if you captivated the room
Or played it even fucking faster.
I still couldn't hear it,
I was slipping out of my consciousness
From the fifth
Into the sixth dimension,
Did Picasso have a purple phase,
Or is it just my singular intention?
Memories rustic in a hotel room,
Hustlers moved online
And became women in their lingerie,
Yesterday and today expect the act of swoon.
Cleaning up which feels rare,
Same as sweeping the August leaves
Off your porch.
Sloppy idea
While your husband was elsewhere
Having a double dip,
Don't tell me that pretentious words
I couldn't find in my dictionary
Was coincidental,
Peonies are worthless
To a botanist.
The lenses we see the world
Are different,
I'm just an obtuse judgemental.
Epilogues write themselves,
When epitaphs are more poignant.

Montclare Featuring Giselle Linder

The subtraction of elements
And the origin of Thorium,
Spun sugar produced
By the same bastard's seasons.
Muhammad Ali steps lighting fast,
Did he ever write poetry?
They said my method lacks a synopsis,
I absorb the patience
Before it tesselates into place
With hydraulics.
Ice cream is what makes the summer,
But it's not the same when it's not served by Ana.
I step backwards
And watch the scene implode from the melodrama,
There's speeds that can't be reached
In your hummer.
But seriously,
Why would you want to drive that?
Words all set their exact place
In the auditorium,
Mind blown by either
That woman back in Amsterdam
Or De-loused In The Comatorium.
Ideas replete my synaptic,
Hence why it doesn't seem to run dry,
And if you think it will
I'll recall my writers drumstick.
It's been a minute,
Can I pass the pen,
And have Hemingway's liquid.

Upon withdrawal from the empire, I can look back and count the dregs of dreams we had no further hours to dream that rest at the bottom of some wayfarer's cup –

As though on their laurels.

They took what they paid me for, and questioned what they asked me for, and left no love behind to pool in their wake like foam behind the boat, which in the mind of the child I once was rose up like mermaids from the deep. The child I once was who has been forever put to sleep.

But I am still spending these wandering years clearing a path through the oaks which will cut straight through to the past, counting knee-bruises and chasing long-gone dogs. Where I used to pray for the man or woman who would raise me up

I pray now for one to put me down. Better to take a straight shot than it is to drown.

South Austin

I don't care
What your Nielsen scan-score is,
I own my numbers.
Ask questions to Sonia regarding jiu-jitsu,
Call it a quiz.
Beyond the city I don't know anything.
The A-C isn't helping the heatwave.
Shall we just share a Grey Goose?
Take a sip.
The evening is getting tense,
Bobbypin hair loose.
The air is filling up
With your honey shampoo,
Her eyes reminded me of Alexis Matsen.
Michigan Avenue on date night,
Not my idea,
But it's a pardon.
I try to work
With more than just the average,
You say Hennessy,
Two shots for our next beverage.
I need to get two things off my chest,
I'm socially awkward,
But lexically bonkers.
A mosaic of everything that takes up space
In the inner workings of my mind,
It should take the place of kintsugi,
Elements of gold free to find.
Don't we all have a cynical view of the world?
Didn't everyone read Judge Dredd?

Oriole Park Featuring Mimi Flood

The sixth side of the prism,
is there both wisdom
And warfare inside a schism.
I can't remember which was the first,
The purple laced in along with white,
It happens in bursts.
So sporadic
You could never say it was rehearsed,
Repeating yourself with a lack of nuance,
I wonder what would Bukowski say
If we were to call him from a seance,
I hear your preference
To Plath or Dostoevsky,
The chemistry was lacking electrons.
Honey mustard is the taste
That got you flustered,
Yeah you know the truth
Between the baseball returning to base
With the throws.
Underthinking when drunk,
Picture in my messages
Containing a peach,
With the exception of gas,
Nothing is out of reach.
Why is everyone
Trying to force electric on me?
What will you do
When the lithium runs out?
Will the prices rise
Much like they done with petrol?
I wanted to see how the blank spaces

Look out of place with doubt,
My messages blowing up,
Replying is an art form
So I'm going to pass the pen
And see whatever comes.

I feel like my body is an image/ And all seven algorithms/ Have their eye on me like some kind of prey/ I find it interesting how the world is covered in corpses/ Some are even unmarked/ And we breathe them in as we walk and sit at our desk/ We consume them by squirting ketchup on hot dogs and eating peaches off trees/ They nourish us with their decay/ And we think of nothing of it/ Too devoured in news and inflation and the jobs that don't care about us and the phones glued to our hands like a beating heart/ What if we do a séance but the thing we open is what keeps us from walking through mirrors to other dimensions/ It's our reflection that keeps us protected from the horror but what if this is the wrong side? What if I walk through and dogs lick the blood from my hands and I get new skin.

Brainerd Featuring Melissa M. Combs

I don't need to forgive people,
I struck them out.
Those who thought
They were going to first base,
They couldn't be more wrong,
It's all asinine.
I wanted my words
To float around like incense,
Before sucker punching
You with yet another punchline.
I'm not alone
In a ubiquitous conscientiousness,
Nor a liar,
Quotes from Christopher Columbus,
Luck runs out
When the main weapon is to shout.
Litmus paper wasn't as accurate
As the decimal point in pi,
Now I find myself
No longer able to sleep off
The jet lag when I fly,
Continuous commute,
No time for cessation,
I was waiting on the words
Not the poison fruit,
Snow White, Adam and Eve,
The pattern of the guilty party,
Boring patriarchal narration.
Illuminate the synaptic thoughts fight.
When all I ever seem to get
Is phone calls from you at 3am.

Do tell me, how is the night vision?
As I stay in tune with my zen.
These night visions
Have gone on for far too long.
3am tells me that this love
Mainly just sleeps.
It's dark and it's dead.
Foolish me,
For mistaking its highs and its lows
As the rhythm of a heart's beat.
How could I have been so naive?
The airwaves travel at such relentless,
And rapid speed,
He should have no other choice
But to let the warmth of them
Seep over that heart,
Frozen at -17.8°C.
Or so at least, I once believed.
But when love and the need to be loved
Gets blurred,
We walk into a storyline
Much more dangerous
Than the climate of man's heart.
What am I to do,
When your hunger is not for me,
But to be immortalized
By my chosen form of art?
I am not your Modern day Van Gogh.
This delusion will not taint me,
And I will not succumb to these hallucinations,
As your clever banter shape-shifts into screams,
Demanding, "Paint me."
I am a poet; an artist, not a god of eternity.
If you wish for everlasting life,
Seek the stars,
Scan the scripts, ask the moon.
But your days with me are numbered.
This ink is drying soon.

Did I mention too, that I am human?
Beneath the sonnets,
And the alliteration,
I feel I am still just a young girl
Fighting through the thoughts
Of complete and total annihilation.
But you couldn't see the soul.
You saw the words.
I wonder what you'll see now,
Because the words,
They've run out.

Brickyard

Any poet stepping to me
Should know,
I'm sending missiles back.
My original intention was neo-poetry,
The stylus scribbled so fast
It perspired relentlessly,
Inspired without comprehension,
The blank stares and black stars
Absorb the rivers
In the patient regulators section.
Eavesdroppers occupy the noise
So much it overbears all actions,
Are we now at an incredulous impasse?
Is it too much to ask
For one night to have court-side seats
Relax away from the continuous cipher,
I just want to sit
And watch Alex Caruso.
As the riots happened in 68
The word Chi-Raq was 2009
And hadn't been said prior.
Now from all the pressure of life
We live by lexical symbiosis.

Pill Hill

Get up at the speed of light,
Polymaths of rhythms
That fight to astrophysical jets.
Jazz musicians
With the ability to recall my level of debts,
Even after all the drugs
Are what got you fucked up,
Messed up
So far passed the nervous sweats.
Retiring the same number twice,
Does it mean
That its value is double the price?
Everything lining up
Behaving like a thousands sixes
Working together in a single line,
Constantly looking like peeling onions,
Pointless,
Though recollecting its function.
Either dark or ruby chocolate
In the breakfast menu,
I don't know the end results
If technicolours breathed life
Into these gentrified streets.
The cure to what you wanted
Hasn't yet become a thing,
Now the lights coalesce
In the summer storms.
When my final thought
Before the daily death decision,
Is how many secrets are lost
On the floor of Lake Michigan.

Sauganash

It's an outdated moment
For us,
Now let's drive the Cadillacs,
Let's steal ourselves a Buick,
Drive towards the morning sun.
Lost somewhere
Inside this monologue
Around page thirty-seven,
I didn't acknowledge
Your pisspoor comeback.
Not unique,
Simply working outside of this algorithm,
Blasé to life
Away from the words I speak,
Eros or Mephistopheles,
Norma Jean charming,
This should have been added
For book burnings,
European cars,
Tattoos not the premise
For receiving or paying
For a lap dance,
Fashion starts in the north,
And propagates as it transpires
Like a knife or fork.
I didn't ask
So don't give me a translation to kabuki,
Decay ambiguous,
A woman's curves that become a fever dream.

West Garfield Park

I was halfway through a thought
Before it switched to you,
Baby it's corridors,
I follow
Before the ejaculation of glitter.
Scrawls inside a furnace,
Carbon blisters hidden
Behind first parchment,
Then plasters.
And if you really think
Austerity isn't a thing
Then let's both walk around the south side,
Or see who leaves
West Garfield Park alive.
And if you really think
This isn't a hustle,
Understand this puzzle,
I won't even give you all the pieces.
And even if I were to feel better,
The queens who were in pictures on my wall,
Should be icons the world over,
And the oscillations
Start from the bedroom floor.
That's only because
It's the location of the fan.
Now let's bounce the idea around,
Shooting twos and threes,
Spaces in the pocket,
Closer than the timing from bottle rockets.
A set of rollerblades not including
A Phoebe Bridger's sample,
Now the words eluding
My haunted house with a picket fence chapel.

While the alcohol
But vegetarian lifestyle acted as a paradox,
You just didn't get it
Hence your automatic car,
And worthless gearbox.
Both sides of the poem read out,
Ignored back
To an out of synch metronome vowed.

Mount Greenwood

I don't know if you were telling the truth
That you were Jimmy Hoffa,
I doubt it.
I can't tell if when I return
It's New York or Atlanta, Georgia.
We'll see where when the time is right,
The exploitation provided was guided
To the fight.
Now when we write it's Chatham
Next to the south side,
Infatuated with the gentrification
Not given to us all.
Flowers that died to express love,
Doesn't make sense or enough.
Fish tanks sitting on Chrysanthemum,
The ideas I had
Are close to the maximum.
Word is bond,
From my neighbourhood,
You know what I mean
Where I'm from,
Understood?
Whereas my stoned therapist or hairdresser
Informed me that
Bad biscuits makes the baker broke.

West Elsdon

Pressure builds on this
Like a synopsis,
It curls inwards before out
Reminding me of the bruises
With precipice.
While the honey you used to wash your hair
Didn't attract anything
But wasps and killer bees,
It was a swarm.
All day breakfast on the menu,
I wanted to secretly know
Your pleasures,
Lipstick curfew,
And bootcut jeans that crack
In the light storm.
We find ourselves with this chemistry
Reverting back
To how we never crack under pressure.
Now the glitches seem to happen,
Like the intervals
Between the arms of The Vitruvian Man,
Patch all of this together
On the beach by Lincoln Park.
North side ideas weigh too much
For me to afford,
Not regarding all these possible proclamations,
I own my home,
Blood, thoughts,
But fall short on other combinations.
Now with the moments I inhale,
Remembering escape is impossible,
So I guess we're all in hell.
Now tell me,

Heaven, hell and purgatory.
Have you ever thought deep
With regards to the parallels
Between the three?

Schorsch Village

I was all out and ready to starve,
When I got a taste for vegan shawarma,
I hadn't eaten meat
Since the times I was in London.
I left the kebab house
And the landscape
Had become a tundra,
Just to step back inside
Would be a panacea,
Now I'm reminded
Of a working girl in Amsterdam
Named Catalina.
The things that she told me
While she prophesied,
It didn't include European gas prices
Meaning we can never be
Privileged enough to switch to electric,
And even if we could,
They'd raise the prices to a new metric.
Closed cities still exist,
We just have to work on conjecture,
Don't take my numbers as a guide,
I'm so far from fucking average,
No school unlike a plane without a propeller.
Charles Lindbergh still holds more relevance
Than Rush Limbaugh,
Though neither
Are as important to me as Tony Stark.

Streeterville

Can you see how all these universes coexist,
Here I am,
Self assist,
Now I have plans away from an adulterous tryst.
I'm not married,
Not in this,
Maybe I can relocate myself
To the dimension
Where they didn't sell Javier Baez.
I understand
Lessons aren't always fully instructive,
While the flowers in her dress
Are way too lavish.
Need a ride,
Which neighbourhood?
Streeterville,
I'll drive you,
I'm not one to pussyfoot.
Why wouldn't you take Ukrainian Village?
What are you scared of?
It being eastern bloc
And they hold the intention to pillage?
No words quite like scrimshaw,
The pure premise of a thesis
Is to teeter on a seesaw.
I'm far away from the idea of being speechless,
Though I don't know
That I'd constitute to Phoebus.
Do the voices inside her head matter
In the same context as Socrates?
I wanted to tell her I'm there, but I'm not.
The bruises on my left leg
Will eventually turn grey,

And I'll be lucky if I wake up on my bed.
It's not bad,
I've had worse days and better tomorrow's.

Wacławowo

Breathe in
The recycled pheromones of the streets,
The man in front of me
Has distorted tattoos,
Mine are hidden
While the waitress compliments my shoes.
The white noise happening somewhere
Distracts me from the J Dilla beats,
The same beats playing in my head.
I fell into it all happening,
David Blaine card tricks,
Blacks and reds.
I'm still broke,
And a rising cost of living,
It's constant dark days
In a financial depression
Disguised as a living cost crisis,
Overpopulation
And the era of personalised face masks
And novel viruses.
A political disaster we had been gestating,
You know how Cancel culture
Has ruined comedy shows
For longer than anyone cares to actually say,
It's not like back in your day,
Still they weren't good.
I know, I know like Bill Withers,
A sleep twitch when running with scissors.
As these are the final hours
Of whatever age I am today,
I count years,
Just not days.
And the philosophical outlook

That the world is full of guitars,
Still there's only one Pat Smear.

Hegewisch Featuring Rhys Campbell

While the isotopes fall apart
How things did in 1999,
It was all so fragile
With the questions asked towards
A beautiful mind.
Terraforming pitchforks
From barely established atoms,
A nine coloured chess board
That stops making sense
With the luxuries of that album.
They wanted the words,
But not those that the south side combined.
Bismuth half-life
Is longer than eternity,
Even if you rounded it out to the nearest third.
And the fine rain that falls
Reminds me that autumn is moments
From happening,
This is again a tangent of my ramblings.
Meanwhile,
The trepidation of this austerity circle
Isn't something we did ask for.
Anagrams with double meanings
Thinking you're clever,
When you never understood
Either Fugees or the score.
Robert Johnson at the crossroads,
Pass the pen
And write on outdated banknotes.
Upon reflection,
What is conformity?

A scratch at the surface of the truth.
Peeking under the veil will drive you insane,
But isn't a slip from sanity kinda beautiful?
I find myself escalating to new planes
When connecting with like-minded individuals.
The ones with a deep belly laugh,
The ones who live freely
And the ones who question the nature of reality
And its intricacies.
No matter if you sit
On the left or right
Of the eagle's wing,
No matter if the baggage you hold
Will break scales;
You are welcome to sit at our table.

Kenwood

It takes a minute
To navigate through,
But those who can survive
Without a signal fire,
Stigmata falling from our own dichotomy,
Cut and chopped down
Reminding me of Victoria Secrets lingerie,
Yesterday that was lust,
Today biology.
Tooth difficulty easy,
Are you telling me
You like the woman who wears clothes
That are boujee ratchet?
Picking up your feeling from the floor
With assistance
From the positive side of magnets,
While the negative exposes
Repressed bruises.
A lack of resistance
From vegan food being delicious,
With the trend exploitation
Obvious still tofu and avocado
Are the definition of nutritious.
I forgot these words,
Or at least my original inserts,
The pieces started to fit together,
And when someone
Pointed out that we made it,
I didn't realise
Because much like Joseph Heller
I already had enough.
But I don't know
What my level of enough is.

Cragin

The six elements of life
That I knew were in existence,
Action of polyrhythms
Along with lines in the ground
Deceiving the eyes of chickens.
Block party strong,
Here the destination of a tattoo belongs.
The fractions of time
Now need to explain
Why they should not be able to fall in reverse,
Poetic spoken entropy ideology,
Ergodic sanskrit predating Deuteronomy.
The probability of cells
That regenerate themselves
Is as close to one
Except in death
When it's worse.
We shouldn't forget anything industrial,
Drums pulsate,
Moving the air non pictorial.
A monolith of this idea
A diva disguised as a mermaid.
My vegetarian ideals
Never feel too constraint,
Meat lacks the soul to be able to liberate,
Do my ideas want to be placed
On a pedestal or shelf?
I doubt it.
The truth to wealth
In life
Was to find happiness and love,
While at peace with yourself.
I work like tomorrow forgot to exist,

The truth is
I think so much I forget how to sleep.

Armour Square Featuring Daragh Fleming

My ideas had become politicking,
They hadn't understood the soufflé
To what's being said
And that's what's contradicting.
I don't know how else to explain
That we are just arms at the edge
Of this spiralling universe,
I'll drive these ideas
With the power of a hearse.
Destruction for dysfunction
And I put the world to rights
With a loving God,
We all wore purple, white and black,
Would you mistake us with goths?
Pianos and guitars,
Broken and smashed up
Like a Cobain Fender Jaguar.
Pyrotechnics for dramatic effects,
When the drunken God
Has no qualm with heretics.
And I wasn't sure about wolves,
Virginia or introspects.
My book contains a lexicon
Thrown out so indirect.
And told to believe the words
From our government,
I'm too distracted by the smell of blondies,
So pass me the oven mitts.
But please only call this an exercise
In our own warped self awareness.
Tell me did I miss anything?

Opening up
Feels like burning your palate - unintentional.
Room-temperature sadness turns cruel
When left to boil.
Is there anything as lonely
As a Sunday evening?
Try a thousand of them on for size only
To find they fit as perfectly as pear-shaped
Jumpers on a body falling into disrepair.
When did all of this happen?
In the dark is the only time we
Remember painful things
We've purposefully forgotten.
Rejection is the most casual of evils
We all commit to.
By design, day-in, day-out,
The perpetual despair
Of the Sunday evening,
Punctuated by all the texts
You never send me.
I remember when you used to like me.
It was around the same time
That I liked myself.

Dearborn Homes

All falling in microscopic mind-hive
Collapse at the seams,
Arms dealers
Who connect with quasar intricate beams,
Perhaps a Tesla death ray.
Can you tell the difference between that,
And the great cosmic ballet?
With all these wonders,
Why are we trash men or hostage,
Robin Hood posses his knowledge.
Looking beyond the boundaries
Of new speak, twin peaks,
Sit together
George Orwell and David Lynch drink.
Bounce ideas count to twenty-five,
It's all dystopian,
We can't all survive.
South side made me,
Was I ever normal?
I wasn't interested in your offers for sex,
Even if it were oral,
A preacher from the Iberian,
Believing every word they spoke
From their Gideon.
Expiring thoughts
That are breaking a sweat,
Has everything been accomplished
On boards ouija or a fret?

Altgeld Gardens

I had my thoughts on the west side of my brain,
I sometimes refer to that
As the pharcyde,
She said I think too much,
Such passages without satisfaction
Have a cessation
That died.
A muse in a faceless thought spirited away,
And here we couldn't contemplate
What we originally knew
And subsequently became a mistake.
No story goes untold,
We all have a gossip in our wake.
Act like they're interested,
But in not understanding
The sonder of the universe
And how it could all be adjusted.
A world lacking Selina Kyle
Or Michelle Pfeiffer
Isn't what I want,
The premise to the cipher
Created by The Riddler,
Forgotten undertones from Thriller,
Polycentric ideas that lost track of time
As they became tantric.
The devil in the white city,
Purple references
And the ideas filthy.
Words like tradition are so outdated,
It was latter day capitalism,
Specks of metal in the dust.
The neon wilderness,
And all these realisations

That purple doesn't belong on the skin
But it looks so apt.

South Loop

Petals that demand control,
And believe me when I say
That I know this is true.
No plane crashes tail-first,
Death doesn't care who's in first class.
Life is rolling entropy
And what the fuck does it care for an impasse.
I am often left fixing my hair,
Not to impress anyone,
Who is there
When I'm in a state of need to repair?
Ready players one,
Two,
Three,
Four;
Juxtaposed without Wi-Fi,
So the austerity means
We're forced to choose
What we should sacrifice
To ensure our futile survival.
Colours that prevent tattoos
From being monochrome,
The original idea was on overload,
Can we spend a night out in Sleepy Hollow?
Insomnia brought out
Some intertextuality I wasn't aware of,
Spider plants and their terrarium seen in macro.
I try not to sabotage my tranquility
Because the chaos of my mind
Is a more familiar terrain,
I establish with myself
I'll be there later.
Sunday was made to be a lazy day,

But I almost never have a moment
To stop and stare.
I guess that's just my nature.

Marquette Park

It could have been a dehydrated question
Which didn't start or end
With a word like me.
The bottle neck approach
Of speak when you're spoken to,
Antiquated more so than the bourgeoisie.
Underwhelmed by the mothership,
Tell me what else was there
I was born to miss?
I got out of bed late
And lost motivation like an arrow,
It was less than half,
My neighbour said cuidado,
I didn't know what it meant.
I guess that's the fear of waking up
To ushanka instead of a SnapBack,
And the questions I ask about myself
Suppressed.
The earliest example of tattoos
I would like to study,
When I'm reminded
That we should be proud of heritage,
That seems arcane,
Breathe the ocean,
Remember that the word follow
Is a suggestion and not an order.

Lilydale

Trees planted in London,
I don't know how they are progressing,
Nothing is overnight,
Even ceramics take time in the oven.
Can you tell me if metaphors
Aren't found in a ninety-five cubical
Locker or shrink?
I racked up air-miles
Without a corporate stroller,
suit and tie,
shirt that's salmon pink.
I was told being verbose was pretentious,
Whereas if I were algebraic
Are they signs to make you jealous?
Please don't describe a job
As being a socialite,
Tomatoes and cabbage thrown
With the intention
Of hitting the playwright.
I smell Shea butter
But I can't give an exact location,
Like the truth from words
Being said by the government.
What is the verity from the bruises,
Look beyond the hive mind
And into the coven.
People wanted shoes
Red and blue,
I stuck mine together
With a purple adhesive
Between the waffle and side of my shoe.
Bazooka tasting digging through crates
For samples in books

That I could use,
Not scratched
As I don't care if I'm caught.
Tongue tough taking tortiglioni,
When we'd rather be tasting linguine.
Sleeping as a moment of clarity
Unaware of the sunspots,
The important atoms
That became evident in a snapshot.

Vittum Park

The local government posts signs
Reading post no bills,
The irony of it leaves me shook still.
Polaroid murals
Yielding postcards exhume qualities,
Groceries laid out in an isosceles,
Along with the truth
Of covered up global atrocities.
The exploited price of life including tampons,
A necessity not luxury like a futon,
Outdated jars of Grey Poupon.
As our brains are fried,
Working towards atrophy,
The truth in the words of my infracted sanity.
Did I tell you how I sometimes hear voices
That I occasionally mistake
For the ones in my head,
Chupacabra,
Slender man,
Serotonin,
And a mixture of the other living dead.
I hear how a voice transpired
To the third base plate.
The calmness of Lake Michigan
Can be felt on the rooftops
Of Waveland Avenue on game day,
A multitude of words stacking up,
Grand Master Flash ideas
Close to the edge,
Transient moments
That patent themselves a wedge.

The Gap

I wasn't sure on the winter idea,
It's still downhill
When the bruises show up here.
I had lost interest with the sex,
Maybe I needed Medea.
Could I just need something
New playing on the deck.
I told the last hypochondriac
To take their feelings with them,
The door wasn't far enough,
And my writers block,
That needs to take itself out the door
Also.
Perhaps I should return my thoughts
To sender,
These bruises still feel tender,
The nocturnal pragmatism
Should muse on a stripper.
When all I need
Is the cousin of death,
A stylo that maybe only to me
Just about makes sense,
Nosedive and the pink light,
The blue lake in the present tense.
Big step into the worldwide,
Adolescent words,
I no longer keep memory
Of the colours of life
Today seem to have split themselves
Into thirds.
I woke up in an arcane room,
There was only Hennessy,
I needed vodka,

More than a sip.
A new woman was in my jeans,
She filled them out,
She took a picture,
Airdropped and returned
As I declared queen.

Crestline

The continuous fake as fuck reward,
And when I wake up tomorrow
Will there be another warlord?
Though the bruises split
And the taste of metal fills the room.
When a sextet tries to regard itself
As a sestina,
The remnants stay
Like burning candles Serpentina.
A pound of flesh smouldering
Could have been
A Jeffery Dahmer all day breakfast,
Changing rabbits to doves inside a hat
Is a trick that's the rarest,
Like scoring a home run
Against a Hoyt Wilhelm scream pitch.
Let the bastards speak
Like salesmen and the wisdom of time
Outside the mind,
He profoundly fucks lost for work
And eating as we see these matrix glitch.
The prism of everything,
It all happens with these aspects of time.

Archer Heights

A switchblade kept together
Worn and in need of sharpening
To remind me of a cutthroat razor,
Asking for a priority pleasure.
A stop start
In the words I wanted to say,
The lucid time we contributed
Away from being able to measure.
Blacked out words
Said by Dr Richard Kimble,
No answers were making sense and I unravel
While hunger occupies my mind.
I was lost within my mind,
My thoughts should have been
On getting onto the purple line,
I didn't know where to stand,
There's a puddle
Containing vomit on the tracks,
The night isn't over,
So take two steps back
As the train is approaching,
I was going to Woodlawn,
What if it were South Shore?
Someone is taking photos
Using the exit sign for lighting,
Mayhaps they consider themselves IG famous,
My brain went back to before
The distraction.
I need to message you about something else,
When I really want to ask,
Can we fall asleep on the couch
To Spirited Away,
You can explain the spell

When crossing the bridge
In holding the breath,
I want to understand,
I don't want anyone else to see you,
Also.
I haven't learnt to articulate my faults,
But you just asked me to show you my new tattoo.

Chatham Featuring Christina Hennemann

The outcome of this gentrification
Will leave us eating the same fucking food,
Ramen noodles.
I'm not complaining,
I put together fifteen of the best
Into a single chapt,
A synopsis so vague
It misses the point like a witches tit,
My geolocation determines
If I wear
My north or south side SnapBack.
The nature of words
And the root of if they even give a shit,
Evolved corrupt and truth
In self worth,
Did I feel that I could have been locked in
With undiagnosed synaesthesia,
Could be pheromones
From mescaline and tequila.
Barmaid asked what I wanted,
Answer oh so simple,
Neither.
Back and forth dreadlocked together by the hair,
A dovetail joint
Which keeps the corners in place
During a game of solitaire,
An idea that shouldn't fly solo,
Cheat codes in poetry matches unlimited ammo.
Pass the pen before sitting in reflection.
I'll have a shot of manifestation magic,
And for him too,

You're never too old
To suckle on a witch's breast.
The world is going down,
Down into history
And her story and no story.
Cling onto every lip and nipple
You can grasp.
Mother earth doesn't love us anymore.
Solve the riddle,
Tom.
Crack the snakes open and pour poison,
Drink it,
Gulp it,
Metamorphose into a skeleton
Until you're thin enough
To slip through the Matrix.
Let's leave this bar,
This street,
This world and soar in solitude.
Just a minute,
Before the news comes on at eight.
Post a picture from the clouds,
See how it turns into a virus.
Rough landing on the feed,
Another catastrophe bombs my sense of fear.
I excel at assimilation,
Embrace this assassination.
And you,
You stay calm or misty
In the dew of dusk- ink a burned star
On your manifestation list;
Rip the nib of your fountain pen
Through mine.

Sheffield Neighbors Featuring Eleanore Christine

The perspective of age and culture
Lessons from school,
I don't remember
Nobody explained the crimes
Of Columbus or Magellan.
I am so lost inside my books,
Outdated medium
Not even for attention.
The diary of a madman
Covering up burns,
College or universities wonder
How you can't study and make something
On a topic they say
Debt should be your true profession.
I started at half-past midnight,
Mining my brain
As if it were lignite,
Pain in the trigger of a gun,
Tagged spray can,
Passion emits itself,
I can count on one hand
The memories I had before I was twelve.
Graffiti murals
Walking south from East Rogers Park
Down to the central underpasses of the loop
Here in Chicago.
Nothing left to my ideas
As they are all dried up from guano,
And all the lines I forgot
Because I couldn't get to a pen,
So now I waiver the hoodie

As you're watching yourself boogie
In the mirror as a distraction
From the menstrual.
There are often things that seem like paradoxes,
Odd socks
That are grey and purple shaded asexual.
Things fall into prejudices,
Would you rather be a prostitute,
Or live outside the zeitgeist
Within the four stars of the city,
The sixth line of a nonagon of solitude?
Ripped out clothes
That are beyond thrifty,
The pen is passed.
Picked up by a new prophet
Who writes the future in smoke
And plastic and bullets sprayed in schools and synagogues
But no one heeds the warning,
Too busy avoiding the old gum on the sidewalk
And each other to notice.

Ranch Triangle

To drive with my favourite in shotgun,
This new ride
And to die with a someone.
The rain happened all night,
And I was misinformed
As to Mars being in retrograde.
And with the spasms
The level of enough
You know it should have been implied,
Metro card discarded
Along with the silver handed over to Judas,
Even you Brutus.
Derelict buildings in these crowded places,
Who was it that used to say I was bipolar?
Tooth decay mixed the blank words
That anguish too much to imply,
Crimson in the sky
When I think either writers block or ammunition
Is servitude to my demise,
Chicago Ridge passing lights
In the rear view mirror,
Dehumanised mistakes
Assume that a human race should be robots.
Fulfilled major notes mixed with minor,
Now I guess the only thing to do
Since this accident is persevere,
Bless Hail Mary residue
Of the vodka last night,
I taste it on your lips,
Belvedere.

Longwood Manor

The candle lights help me relax,
My mind needs a minute
As the wax melts loosen themselves,
Nutmeg and lemon that fall into place
Filling the room.
The room full of butterflies,
The collector,
And the infatuation with Miranda,
Shame her letters were never delivered.
Was I even aware of epistolary?
Did the word make its way
Into my dictionary?
The blacked out street lights
Of Lake Shore Drive,
Power cuts during latter day capitalism
Is becoming the norm.
Executing
A global glasslike gentrification,
Not everyone has the resources
To remain warm.
I wanted to be remembered
For more than just the bruises
On the skin of me,
Again I iterate
Not to research my teeth,
I'd simply be a John Doe
Lacking identification.
A step, ball change
To my dust collecting Ibanez,
I hold no intentions with a Flying V,
I'll explain it vidartes.
I don't think everyone understood,
I wasn't trying to save the world,

I just needed to have enough
For myself
To navigate through.

Lavergne Avenue

Cook it up,
The relaxed moment
Before I remember there's a dystopian reality
If you have the ability to wake up.
Peg leg while I endure this
Through braggadocio and petrichor,
Not the best option,
But it beats unwanted liquor.
She didn't want to listen
To my algebraic rambles,
Amalgams fall out as I try to explain how,
I wasn't anti political,
Just anti intrusive
As should anyone else be,
It wasn't always like this,
Now that just seems mythical.
The strained look of subjects
In this totalitarian state,
Now a protest march
Doesn't have the same effect as cornstarch,
Nothing changes until the ideas get radicalism
In the roots of its bloodstream.
I guess there's too many millionaires,
So raise the prices,
Paper planes,
Where's the new Butch Cassidy?
I guess this is the end of humanity,
I say it like anyone should be surprised,
Or consider it a tragedy.

Homan Square Featuring Ashley Roncaglione

What about all the notes in diaries
Written when drunk
And they were forgotten
Like the words I wrote
About the pain I had in chemical burns
When I was back in London,
It didn't matter if my eyes
Looked at the Seine, Thames, Amstel
Or when I get to see the Hudson.
A dive bar with a stranger,
The drunken ramblings from the other end
Was barely legible.
Then again,
My hearing isn't as sharp as a razor.
Wait a minute,
Did they have the intentions
Of creating a barroom brawl?
What did they say the name of this place was?
I came to Bernice's for inspiration,
And the words follow the leader,
Here all sounds get drowned out,
I heard the notes of a piano,
But it wasn't Billy Joel.
We got more drunk
As I tried to explain the rules
Of you pay fiasco.
D'angelo off key
All sounds like the quantising
Would have ruined it,
A parallel to life,
Drive to maintain,

Off from swing,
Dilla feels and wings,
Make or understand just don't contrive.
What did you see?
What about all the names written on napkins
The sweat from my whisky glass seeping
Like the words they spoke to me about salvation
Now the numbers and words keep bleeding together
Is that a 4 or a 9?
Doesn't matter.
My vision isn't keen to retrieving
And I wouldn't have called anyways
When you think scripture is light reading
Feeling light
Light bending
Far sight
Sight slipping
Always tip the barback
All words with no meaning
Do we live to survive
Or survive without thinking
Your face is distorted
I'll tell you what I'm seeing

Desplaines Street

Did anyone even listen
When I had transcended
Into my own soliloquy,
The holes that multiply
Within the mind,
The drawing of a line
For either side of the contingency.
I study the moves of an old man
As he plays chess,
I asked him what his play was
In six moves time,
Vaguely his tone said
"Guess."
His trash talk in between moves
Didn't make sense,
A myriad of strokes,
Reminding me of Mr. Miyagi teaching lessons
In painting the fence.
Now I can't tell the difference
Between offence and defence.
His philosophical teachings
Burnt through the placenta of time,
The elements of food and sleep
Which need to be confined.
To be honest with a lack of interest in money,
While understanding economy,
Watching botany
And life grow outside the trammel
Of this ecology.
An observation I saw
Between the Bishop, the pawn,
And the clock that stopped was,
The wisest person in a room

Isn't ever the one who speaks the most,
I asked one cryptic question,
Can you see the tattoos on that of a ghost?

Bowmanville

I didn't get a message from a woman
That normally exposes smut,
There's a grip to how she does things,
Don't tell her husband
She made me bust a nut.
Informing me
That he doesn't write on my level,
He could travel to Alpha Centauri,
Overdose on coffee,
It still wouldn't be helpful.
When it appears
That there's logic to the understanding
Of land masses,
I wasn't sure if it applied to this metropolis.
There's a sewing machine collecting dust
Ready to be weaved,
Could there be a way of knowing?
Even if we beefed?
Meanwhile,
A woman that spoke about
Her untapped potential,
Reciting corruption,
L. A. Confidential.
She opened up more
As her mouth was covered by her hand,
Said her husband was born as a nomad,
From an unrecognised land.
Where? I asked,
The deserted nothingness of South Sudan.
I asked about the reason to be candid
While also discreet,
Always pay cash,
Remember not to bog life down

With unwanted receipts.
Bio freeze the inception of ideas for currency,
And the truth of this double tripolar
Not written in the terms and conditions,
Maybe it was invisible ink,
It could have been truth when they said
It was written.

Fernwood

I was just a depressed disciple
Deep in Dilla,
Unable to recreate the beat patterns,
So I applied the liquid
To my syntax knowledge.
My daily message from Bonello
And melting wax nutmeg and lemon,
Evening transcends to
French Vanilla.
Tensegrity seems to work
As a word I can't articulate,
I have streams of words
In my head
And I go for the drawing of lots.
Meanwhile I don't have the answers
That my brain is after,
And I'm constantly
Looking for the godshots.
While the cysts
Just sit dormant in your hands,
Cupid in a paradox
Sleeping upright,
Muted with a docks equinox
Leaving receiving contrite not provide.
In the winter
We could drive up north,
You said that you wanted to listen
To Oliver Stone,
His wisdom in the wilderness
Is close causing me to smack him
For lying again.
How many greats would you say
Are a first draft pick?

I feel the witness of what you say
In these deep blues and bruised purples.

Bucktown

An examination that we progress to more,
Just to struggle
When we need to fall back.
And a china doll that sees life
From the outside,
Resisting a pre-existing moment
That happened outside the limits of Kodachrome.
These spirals of nothingness
In the astronomy of life and time,
Purple nightlights with no sense of direction
As to where is home.
Can the aurora borealis
Reach this far south?
The data spinning like a vinyl
I don't have the setting for,
In information trapped within dark matter,
Energy in chaos
That could take a minute to settle,
Or even forever more.
It was so much more surreal than a dream,
I wake up remembering
You having Elizabeth Olsen hair,
Unsure if it were a dream,
I couldn't decipher the couple in the loop
For all I know it was khmer.
A Shakespeare play that didn't touch on demise,
Notes out to the universe;
Waiting more than a lifetime on the reply.

Kelvyn Park

It's a small wonder
How the world progresses,
Shapes and the post
I send my mother won't get to her,
Not on time at least.
A fake action to astronomy
And the misconception of plexus.
Now my mistakes
Feel like grammatical errors,
Finite staying awake
For the moment we can afford to breathe,
Do you know
What could be considered truth?
In these lawless times,
The national guard totalitarian
Silence
Between the atrocities and crimes.
A theory that goes all the way up
To J. Edgar Hoover.
Couldn't find the time
To tie my laces,
What ever happened to those kicks
From Back To The Future?
Guess my slip on vans
Will go with me to different places.
So now these thoughts seem to stray
Like a house cat,
Roaming the city
And can't find his way back.
Now I have spasms
As I walk away from my thoughts
That contained something resembling you,
Inhale, exhaling

Through the bruises
Of a former lucid dream.

Back Of The Yards

I was waiting
For the fabric of time
To move backwards,
And entropy to reverse
Or do what it doesn't.
The levels of emotions found in echoes,
Memoirs sound healthy
Even with the purples and the yellows.
I saw it all in so much space,
In between the skin,
Prefabricated whispers possibly knowing
They were almost nothing to the universe
Apart from lies committing sin.
Now I choose what I chose,
And the conscious poetry I was after
Didn't exist outside my mind,
Now nothing seems to juxtapose.
I know, I know,
Everything nowadays is a paradigm,
With perfect alignment
Tempered through iodine.
Forever shouldn't have been this.
So say it to yourself,
Some people don't know
The right moment to change,
And when they do
It's too late
Remember the manic Indian summer?

Calumet Heights

Lamborghini's are for the rich and racketeers,
I'm a 2008 BMW 1 Series at best,
The seance I met you at
Seems to now have spaces,
Is space even for the final frontiers?
Now I steal serotonin from Godzilla,
Copy and paste gold chains
Traded for ramen,
Now look at me with your left eye closed,
Now the photographer
Wants us in a Ratjakowski pose.
Now a cyclops eye
Isn't lacking a phantom altercation,
Tiptoe in the conversation
Before the buzzer
Understand the rules to operation.
Now we're so far from strangers,
Because of Rheign on a blue day
My SnapBack represents the Texas Rangers.
Even though
I normally represent the south side,
A change does me good sometimes.
An idea
That you thought was kinda strange,
Remember there are delinquents
Who only see
A flat earth and deny climate change.
Compromised by models in lingerie
And non electric whips,
You'll be infatuated
By how she rests it above her hips.
I've confessed too much,
I need a straight moonlit vodka

Twisted with lime,
No longer do I now speak Dutch.

Galewood

I still see the parallels
Between life and hell
And I always maintain,
I wouldn't recognise the person
I should have been.
It's not always down to design,
Blackhawks jersey with zirconia,
But it's not what was envisioned
Obscured by wine.
I started to remember
That I was feeling healthy,
I was looking for a better tomorrow,
We gave each other
Good Days by SZA,
The downstream view
As we rest with the golden hour
Of the river.
The faint trace of your lipstick
Was now on my lips,
It was where your impulse
Contorted with my relationship,
And to hide
The hidden conflict.
Now,
The scent of paradise
Flows through the city streets,
Before it's whisked away,
Decor remains,
And I don't know the layout
Of any penthouse suite.
But my philosophical outlook today
Was there's no bunk beds in the graveyards.

Lakewood/Balmoral

Tear gas goes up,
But it's worse
When it falls back down,
It's always going down
In the orbs of this town.
Now can you tell me,
Are these pages just my coffin?
A stranger getting off the metro
Said to their phone,
"I'm so deeply lost in my own soul,
How can I expect anyone else to understand me?"
I could relate.
I smell the ideals
From the remnants behind the cigarette smoke,
Now there's hexagrams
Unsure of their own level of false hope.
I approximate the exact time
For an all day breakfast,
And the barflies don't represent the masses,
Even if they think their gibberish
Is putting the world to rights,
I cringed out,
Like I do with people
Who sing with their eyes closed.
Could you please stay quiet
Like Chinatown turtles?
Now all the hoards will see
Is an epitaph that reads
Here lies an insubordinate
Who didn't understand
The concept that everything
Goes full circle.

Loyola

As I sit on the couch
To explain my problems,
It reminds me,
My barber complains
About all my nonsense.
If I had described her words
As a muse,
Would her mind soften?
I didn't know
If the mind could get an appraisal,
Like anything beyond this cipher
Had forgotten
To be left on the writers table.
Guess I should return to steal,
And while the cracks in my hands,
Split to expose more
Than the bruises
Which were already there,
The dried blood
Says nothing more than take care.
The unstable wanting for wanderlust,
I forgot to write down
The shit I saw inside my hive mind,
I wish I could be a little more honest.
Now all I do is work on my feelings,
Sometimes it's therapeutic
To have the candles and steam
Reach up to the ceiling.
House burns down,
As the flames go up,
That's a paradox,
I guess I don't know my silence,
Who said they put the key to the lock?

Kennedy Park

All I hear are the dulcet tones
Of women from Suriname,
And now we can only make it
Halfway away from napalm,
Or their launch codes.
Are the deaf immune to the sounds
As the city
Then world explodes?
I don't get things sometimes.
You say I'm such a nerd,
Seriously when it comes to words,
I'm worthy like James.
Sorry that's the wrong city,
Scott Williams,
I'm staying in the game.
Now I don't get an ice cold anxiety
Over the typewriter ribbon,
I look over at last nights fling
She has her mouth open while applying eyeliner,
These thought patterns don't appear correct
In the first instant,
It reminded me of Primer.
Everything can dwell down with my chi,
A Rickenbacker bass
Dropped an octave
When I couldn't get clearance on a sample,
But I'd use it anyway.
I'm soul searching,
I should have been ignoring my screenplay,
One word at a time working like Hemingway.
Give me a thorny crown of wildflowers,
And they shall find home
But it won't give them solace.

Budlong Woods

The insidious nature of the streets
In the heart of this city,
While Al Capone
Was still in distant memories.
They were people who held grudges,
Life doesn't move
When born under punches.
I had requiems lost in dreams,
Cracks in the skin
When knuckle dusters
Live as clusters
For thieves.
One fucks up the other,
Seriously the midnight shines
So much more in the bruises,
Than when others poke their mouth
With self-indulgent snouts.
Silent moments from boiling potatoes,
I mean poets will retire
Unable to figure all this out,
Like you can count the seconds
And it still won't make much sense.
It's not even the polysemy of rhythms
That happen like spasmodic kick drums,
Dilla time was close,
Though not as intense.
A conversation
That dived down the rabbit hole
Of are wax melts simplified incense.

Portage Park

Life was always
Just a series of non sequiturs.
I wasn't sure
If that even made sense to me.
How is it with you?
Did you think
We could go intercontinental
Without French toast,
I know you want tiramisu,
My fingers still have remnants
Of ramen residue.
If tomorrow was today,
I couldn't tell you
If it were better than yesterday,
Don't pour your breakfast
I remember what you wanted,
Latte.
This can't be real,
It doesn't feel like a dream,
A despot speaks
And the sun disintegrates off his smile,
The only truth he says is,
This is a draconian action
To losing your mind.
Here we feel the whole family shake,
And I hear you say
Bae, bae, baby
Let's just Marie Antoinette and eat cake.
Now the world is wrapped up
With riddles,
I found I couldn't figure things out
With the liquor in my mouth,
And now you look at me,

While the bruises they show,
After dark and all through the night.

Ravenswood Gardens Featuring Joel Anthony Ciaccio and S. Bruzon

Plaid's back in style now
For the first time since the 90's.
The tartan's originally from
The Pacific Northwest: Cobainian,
Periodically blood stained,
Hematocrit levels maintained
As the fads bleed out rapidly from the head.
Torn jeans are ripped on purpose now
And sold at Target. The POS machines up front
Won't accept cash anymore,
But will ask for your phone number instead.
Oh, and vinyl's made a come back too.
You can buy all the reissued soundtracks
These clothes came from. Sweat shops
Will dress us up and keep our heads bopping
To the monotonous beat.
Can you hear it? The stylish lock groove
Of capitalism after the last song
On each side of an LP's black disk,
Where the last word will sound like static.
Where an old pair of Chuck Taylors
Could've saved you some money.
I wouldn't expect you
To associate with
The people that I do,
Half are strippers,
The others are so tight
You could call them either ducks
Or non tippers.
So there's this one woman,
She wears demin raw on her skin,

Ripped during sex
So you know the thread was thin.
Now it was all split reminders
Of seconds and atoms,
So now I call four five four,
The colour of the new car
Is working with a Rolls Royce phantom.
Imagine Godzilla with a machete,
Diving bells
Though passive with a butterfly,
I recall the toxic masculinity,
Don't act like a tough guy.
Try sipping gasoline,
I'm guessing you will mistake it
With acetylene.
Try feeling on her skin,
You will ignite it like amphetamine.
I wouldn't expect you to associate with the people that I do,
Most are nothing,
Nothing like you.

Fifth City

And when you think
This is just about enough,
Twitches over the Adam's apple ending tough,
Stopped with whispers
And watch all this shake up,
Blacked out retro guitar,
Elements added and spasms happen,
Now imagine a movie scene sidebar.
Stop talking,
It's not making sense.
Life could be transposed,
Your words touched my soul
The same way the lyrics did in Dozed.
Now I called on myself
To find distractions,
The bruises are existential humanity elements,
Wait,
Stop,
Pause,
Find a second to rebuild.
Now the ambiance plays muted glockenspiels,
It's a walking contradiction
Wearing their mothers heels.
Did anybody try
Sending out an S.O.S signal?
I feel like I need one right now.
All my vocal interactions
Are based within this guild,
I need what I need,
When I start to say things
Outside my comfort zone
I feel like a cheat.
Now and then I blackout,

When the purple comes across my eyes,
Everything isn't heard,
So when I'm asked to recall
What they said to me,
About last night;
I didn't know
What I was supposed to be remembering.
Are these the moments
When it's best to just admit defeat
For the day,
And resign to the couch?

West Pullman

I don't know
If you needed to hear it,
But I've got unopened bottles of vodka
Older than you are,
I don't know how true that actually is.
So as the ash from your cigarette
Doesn't drop,
That's because of the pin
As a distraction prop.
The homeless don't have the same optimism
As those who stay around
The highway underpasses.
Still what I said
Back on that date with Marissa,
It'll always be
The masses against the classes.
Soon is a case of relocation,
The Wi-Fi's broke,
Though that's not my vocation,
See I don't fully embody
My attitude of woke,
I still embrace derrière models,
And I know the words that I spoke.
Though they were intended as compliments,
I apologise
I'm hungry and today was tempted
By rice over noodles.
Maybe I'm crazy
Does it last more than moments?
Tonight I think I'll sit with the drink
And cogitate the sections of my mind,
Until all the answers
Arrange themselves to the answer of win.

Wrightwood

Pulling the plugs from the mics
And now the words reverberate
Reminding me of a mausoleum,
The crowd said
We should have used swampy words,
I was feeling at a disposition,
Could have been uneven.
Now then,
Black was the colour of home,
While white was love;
I guess that purple really shows pain.
I can't wait for the future
And the nighttime elements
Of my feet in the sand grains.
I didn't want to get distracted
By bureaucracy,
Though in moments of reflection,
I didn't know how to write like Homer,
The Odyssey.
I'm more in a Survival Of The Fittest,
Or Twelve Jewelz,
That describes me.
There are days
When I find myself
Lost in a world that doesn't exist,
So even though I remember
The name of
An old friend,
We don't talk anymore,
But they are still
The greatest of all time
In the back of my mind.

Morgan Park

First base plate,
Gehenna wasn't a vacation
We were on the edge
At a different estate.
Henna tattoo intricate in design,
Hubris as a tessellated idea
Though more refined.
Just sparks
Are all that's needed to stay alive,
While in this city
We blend in and remain nameless,
The same as Ryan Gosling in Drive.
So as there are words that are forgotten
Until death same as Henry Darger,
I try my best now
To not over expose myself
Like an expired film.
I think if I did
I would call it
Poets traumatic stress disorder.
Working on the occupation of my mind
With a grandmother
Who would spend their time
Making verivorst sausages,
While now I struggle to remember
What it was like to live
Without a trilogy of therapists
Who occupy different chambers inside my phone.
So as my thoughts run wild
At half past midnight,
Only place there is a rope
Requested by a sequester,
Would be if I were sat at ringside.

Here we are unsure if tomorrow is the day
We head back to the north side,
When the summer comes,
We should go and check in on Jessica,
I know those bruises on her knees
Have been replaced with tattoos,
But still it would be good
To make sure she's alright.

North Kenwood

I find myself a long way from home,
But I placed a back-masked vinyl
In the place of my heart,
So the ideas started
With poetry being a luxury,
When I realised it's so much more
Than a necessity.
Now I'm terrified
That you could hear the elements
Start to skip,
Is doomsday the countdown to an apocalypse,
Or waking up
To an apparent need for microchips.
I should have stayed home
And opened a bottle,
Instead I was trapped in a coffee shop
Listening to people
Have a shallow deep conversation,
I should've stayed masturbating
To the emotional attachment to a model.
Conscious poetry,
Taboo topic stigmatised socially.
While I focus on the ten-four,
Procrastinating?
Procrastinate but don't back out on me now.
A peninsula at the base of California
That I forgot existed,
Jessica Chastain redhead actress,
Unknown beyond a casting couch;
And the films she forgot to re-record
As the lead in her mind.
Seriously,
Did we all find ourselves

Lost in a reality
That we forget to dream?

Pilsen

Climbing up a mountain faraway
From peanut butter and banana sandwich
Surprise,
But it's a distraction from my original answer,
Guess I'm going to have to say twice.
I don't know if I blacked out,
But this seems to have organised itself
To be slightly different
From the light in this place,
So as today and tomorrow
Feel like better days,
We'll have to wait and see
What Sunday brings.
Remember the depth to my superstitions
And beliefs in karma.
I ordered sixty flowers for a widow,
The spectrum of colours
To decorate her window.
A cyclone which is forgetting
What it means to blink,
Distracting myself when I tell friends
I'm soul searching
To get out of multi person drinks.
My problems are deeper than that,
Just because life isn't exactly
As you thought it would be,
Doesn't mean that trouble
Always falls in threes,
How about explaining everything
You have had out of this existence.
Remember that everything has an inception
And cessation
In the fraction of an instant.

Kosciuszko Park

Allow me to layer my thoughts
On top of each other
As they dry,
It'll remind you of an acrylic,
Could you say if my thoughts
Were spasmodic or realistic.
The grey was supposed to be back in Paris,
There were things there I wish I had kept.
When finding an excuse
That sounded like anything
You'd accept,
A parable
Where the only information gained
Was there are no highways in the sky,
Can you tell me at what point
The sunshine becomes a memory
As a result of how high?
I remember you wearing a wig,
Was it one Vivian Ward would pick?
Did she look better with or without?
Washed sins away
Inside the basilica,
My thoughts submerged in vodka,
A labyrinth,
Now there's a Poliwhirl
Who seems to mirror my fingerprints.
Can you make an effort to be unseen?
The misspelling of the word,
And adding four additional letters
To dingbat.
Fall off,
Falls do happen,
It's how you stand up

After the cuts and bruises
Because prominent.

Burnside

If only this reality
Was all just falling into place,
The nature within matter
Was made of three basic fundamentals,
Solids, liquid and gas,
Relatively only exists
To south side Miles Morales.
A cyberpunk outfit smelling of hair dye,
Sex, and leather jacket.
Johnny Blaze,
Guess it all makes sense on Burnside,
Monastery gospel
I don't need to explain how RZA
Is the abbot.
He had words so sharp,
They could have been misunderstood
As being obsidian.
Notices on billboards
Inform me
That this is little more than a dream,
Moments fall at the wayside
For it's paramount
To make a supreme team
Consisting of more than fifteen.
Sometimes my mind get sidetracked,
Nothing stays in there for long,
It's constantly ransacked.
I saw this thing that said
Life is just collecting guests
For your own funeral.
My reality shattered when I read that,
Not being able to see your audience,
That's the only but.

Hermosa

What if I didn't register
The idea of paradise?
Oh,
And then it was all
An astral projection,
I find myself in a facility
Where I'm the only one
With recollection,
Nobody else still has thoughts
Of Sarah Michelle Gellar.
Wormholes forgotten
While not exploring full interstellar,
Exact nature of which
I didn't proceed,
And it's all a linear process,
Garnished with mustard seeds.
So does that mean
This timeline will break?
And this could all go macro,
But when you disassemble the whole idea
Until it begins to resemble a triptych.
All of this could be wrong,
I know I'm often wrong.
Everything will eventually waste away,
In the same manner
As a Salvador Dali clock,
But for those who want more knowledge
Than they could ever comprehend,
Listing out those with Mephistopheles
And his list of friends.

Heart Of Chicago

Counting the forgotten stars,
Blocked out by light pollution,
I swear that it wasn't like this
In the Hollywood Hills,
Unsure if my words are even proven.
What the fuck,
I'm only human.
Mistakes in what Bryan Ferry said,
It's all just thrills.
How much I need to code switch,
Manipulating the words
Ever since I was a snot nose,
Apricots and liquid honey
Abyssinian crows.
Crawling seductive,
Making the sheets move impulsive.
The music feels lo-fi,
Temperature is getting hot,
Are we all deep fried?
Now all of the sequesters
Fall in and dream of their first bride,
I will try and explain it
In some sort of fashion tonight,
And there were remnants
Of nail polish on the walls
Of the mausoleum,
I don't know the culprit,
But the results are often uneven.
The moonlight has always been busy,
Same as the Cloud Gate,
Would you rather call it The Bean?
Consider this a warning,
I'd rather be late

Than stop listening to Nights
Halfway through,
Because you know sleep is so much more
When you realise
That reality isn't relevant
Or taking score.

K-Town

Did we have anything
To celebrate today?
Baby could you explain
Why you couldn't remember my name?
Would you agree since we went vegetarian,
Ouzo wasn't enough for a liquorice fix.
Honestly I am craving
The taste of sweetcorn
BBQ style, Korean.
I guess a day without Wi-Fi
Would be better for me,
I just needed a moment
To clear my head.
The instrumentals of sounds
Embedded inside my cranium,
I guess I should feel thankful
That life doesn't get too much
For the atriums.
I was sat on the left side
Of the metro as it left the loop,
Is there a numerical difference
Between a group and a crew?
I tried to avoid the political topics,
As I understood the origin
Of left and right.
The door to the coffee shop opens,
And the doppelgänger of a stranger
I'll never know walks in.

Lake View

The unusual answers normally use logic,
But this is portmanteau,
And I'm not rich enough
To use that word.
So in my mind
I recall this working girl from Amsterdam
She had red lingerie and black pantyhose,
But that's not relevant to this optic.
Someone called out the person
On the other end of their phone
For gaslighting,
How many people had I experienced that toxic?
You know,
The vile display of ignorance
And people being obsessed
With self confidence and success books,
All the while keeping their cards
In the pockets of capitalism,
No different from colonialism,
Apart from my cash bought 511's
I am so far off the goddamn grid,
I often forget
How I should pronounce my own name.
So as the highway is full of false indicators,
Material secrets I think I already knew about,
What's the context for calling
Districts of the city dystopian,
I guess I will never be able
To see the sunset over Lake Michigan,
Not at least from the edge of this city.

Eden Green

An institute which fits together
Like my arrogance
Over multiple semesters,
It used to be words,
Now it's under appreciated books,
Candles that I'm the collector.
I'm just a wordsmith
Who never keeps everything locked up
In a briefcase,
Unlike the backpack poets
Prophesying on the purple line of the subway.
I guess my level of envy
Should have been higher,
Brighter lights than the city needed,
What happened to the codes cheated,
I know everything counts down to nothing
Moments that elapse on a timer.
So now things emanate
From the centre of this spiral
In our consciousness
That consists of this universe,
Though I might be wrong
In the nature I observed.
Now I'm unsure,
Did we actually need to make space
For flowers in the city?
Crooked roses grow through
Concrete and asphalt,
Fuck even when life is gritty.
Neptune wanted to skateboard,
Running dripping with this Dilla alchemy.
Alternative stassy pharmacies
Antidote for teenage lust over Kelly Kapowski.

Is there one?
Poetry wires mixing sex, lies, videotape,
How much more before more than my circle
Realise my auteur?

Old Norwood Featuring Josie Eckersley

Important people don't give every piece
Of information when they're explaining
Antiquated configuration,
Food and liquor inspired art,
Speed racing from a hunch
Eyeballing every permutation
Within this juxtaposition.
Those opinions sounded like
Something something Houdini,
Add two carrots to the recipe
With zucchini,
Audacious when the tears and nose
Were both full of snot.
A failed feature,
What was that bae?
You wanted to eat ice cream
As long as it was fully synchronised
With The Matrix fight scenes,
Now I spend my time
With the maddest of all mad hatters,
Selling ideas to digest,
So long as you use a platter.
The vision inside my head
As the words simply splatter,
She wore Tiffany,
Nothing else,
Creating an explosion later.
For now it's a symphony,
With the usual mishearing lyrics,
Thrill her nights.
WHAT DO YOU EXPECT OF ME?

To join your circus mischievously
Without caution or a word of warning?
To surrender to your fire breathing lips
That hang on my shopping list,
To give into your power
And recite every answer to your questions
Like every girl forgets without hesitation.
No I won't let you follow me down
Into my spiral
Or spend your future
Fighting for your survival,
Like you're depending on my bones,
Hanging from my every moan
And spend every last breathe that you own.

Ashburn

Finding bliss in a barrel,
Or double handling throwing tomahawks
As running into battle.
Is an ego made limp
From the words of a Beowulf.
Now I am starting to remember
My peace of mind,
Guess I finally know
What the fuck I actually think.
Palm trees and the gentrification
Taking the taste
Out of ramen noodles and swink.
Now we have garbage
Taking over the city streets,
But this can be ignored at Midway,
Years from now
We can wake up without condensation
On the ideas of shows on Broadway,
Tonight we'll people watch
At the nearest dive bar,
Do you recall last time
That woman plucked from cinema's golden age.
The ancient wisdom and hypocrisy
Before words were written,
With what I do and don't know
It's lopsided piles resembling Neuromancer
Ask for the definition by William Gibson.
A failure In transmission,
Much the same as the lipstick
On woman at the end of the bar.
Was that really a transition?
I count three delinquents
Who can only speak slang

Trying to impress a princess,
Pedagogue lacking the wisdom to truly teach,
Did I really need to know
That either follows each.

Beverly View

The quantum mechanics,
I explain to myself
How I love poetry,
Gospel to the words in therapy,
I wrapped it all up
In sessions for writings.
There were ideas that dig deep
Into the works of Tolstoy or Fyodor's,
Now watch as the idiot fails
In an anomalous motor,
Nothing more than mouth.
Now I see everyone eating
Gold plated steak knockoffs,
Let them polish the social media shine off,
Is it only I who does wonder
The difference in timeline
Without death
For Anastasia and Natasha Romanoff.
Maybe I'll sober up next year,
Perhaps I'm just expecting too much loyalty,
Mayhaps this is the madness of multiples,
No this is.
I could have wanted millions,
But I'd rather be me
Understanding the tree of life
And the branches that exhibit
Each of my feelings.
Now the solitude of the mundane
Elements of life,
Drinking alone in a hotel bar,
Or an office staff party.
Nobody understands how much
I have to fight against the carcolepsy.

Talley's Corner

The cold weather freezes the temptation
And discomfort from the harsh Chicago winter,
Fortunate to having shelter.
The minor things with what she said
How a wise person can play
Both the Shakespearean role
Of a genius or a fool.
Some say to
Take the long road and walk it,
I walked the long way myself,
Now there are imperfections,
I find them in everyday life,
I stopped counting past twelve,
The outside noise
With forgotten words mentioned.
I didn't even drink the issue,
A virtuoso cracked hands
From the cold winter,
Fuck all to discuss
When not looking in the rearview,
Mirror, mirror cracked
And left by each of the Great Lakes,
Does kintsugi help relaxation escalate?
Adolescent lazy eye zero synchronicity
And you expect me to understand
The retrograde words between Mercury,
All the while Scorpio is rising,
It didn't have the desired effects
That you wished,
Much the same as
Mistaking buttercream for icing.

Noble Square

I wasn't after speaking
In my native tongue,
Constructive dialect,
Three out of five,
It's difficult to dig
Without retrospect.
Homage to battered Wi-Fi before circumspect,
A poltergeist or polygon
In my corner holding out that we can thrive.
The colours of wires
Were found in the bloodstream,
Mermaids tonight blinded
With the ideas projected,
Some repeat words
Frozen out of their original context,
I can't always be sure,
Though I'm often suspect.
Remind yourself how dog walkers
Offer their services,
Constantly typing out their own number,
Homemade flyers
And the purpose of persistence.
I wouldn't try to fight the ideas
Had they been black and white,
But they're shaded purple and greys.
And all I remind myself
Of is that on a different day
I didn't feel alright,
Whereas today
I'm tired but optimistic.

Marshall Square

The soul and jazz clubs
At night pulsate with the seconds
Between notes from the saxophones,
Staccato definitions played out,
Laconic style
Through the microphone.
Hubris found at the blues crossroads,
Herbie Hancock and Muddy Waters
Discovered by millennials
On LimeWire illegal downloads.
Crushed the numbers of a dice
So they all started to look ergodic,
When I said my logic,
My thoughts came with vodka tonic,
Straight out the optic.
Often I shut my eyes
And see the outline
Of Libra and Orion,
Idyllic outside the tethering of the mind,
Overpaid Louis Vuitton,
And I see my SK8-Hi Vans
Being stripped away by a siphon.
Waffle on the print
And I'll stay unsigned.
Now I'm never certain about much,
I can say The purple sky
Looks imposed with crayons,
While here the words became forgotten
Somehow similar to the architecture
Of churches.

Bronzeville

I didn't chastise myself
For branching out
Beyond a own level of Ebonics,
I searched the west coast,
Multiple elements of Europe,
And I'm starting to understand
Airplane hydraulics.
Everything falls into place,
Almost as if it were planned by Kate Bishop,
And the moon night metro gossip,
Creole homemade vodka
And leaving in the morning
Without a trace,
So as I'm forever
Trying to find the soul of poetry
In donuts,
And my moments of tranquility
Elapse in banks that house blood,
I'm going to remain
Waiting on the scenarios
To present themselves.
I ask myself out loud,
If I could backmask the truth,
Would I write it down?
Here we keep a shit car
So it doesn't get stolen,
Airplane mode so the call stick to mute.
Ray Charles said it best,
Life is taking time to hit the right notes.

Woodlawn

An emotional profoundment
To how words look
And not so much sounded,
While sometimes my mind
Feels like it's torn apart
The same as mozzarella sticks,
I microchopped and rearranged
Emulating legends
from the forgotten mix,
The previous name of The Chicks,
Infatuation urban paradise graduation
Edge Of Seventeen dance Stevie Nicks.
I get to separate what's personal
From business,
A dark haired woman,
With lipstick tattoos,
Six stringed bass guitar
And a button nose.
Another microchopping session
With images that transfuse,
And here,
Here when I'm by myself
I find my mind starts drifting
Into the ether,
You know somewhere else.
Maybe a paradise to get away to.

Cottage Grove Heights

I'm not the only one waiting
On the warm August nights,
Chicago front porch parties,
Working on the outer reaches
Of the cosmos and other proxies.
Down the street the drunken fights,
I guess it was their turn to relapse.
One day I'll have an apartment
With a lake side view
On the upper east side,
So my only issue
Will be my lack of sleep at night.
Now I have never tripped on money,
But seriously,
What do I know
About the freeze in the Midwest,
Italian cars,
Plasma TV's,
With what came
Between the words
Denied and request.
I miss the salad days of graffiti,
Kick flips
And poetry.
When I left the west coast
I noticed the world had entered a changeling,
And like the time
I listened to Relationship Of Command,
I had reached
A destroyed videotape singularity.

Lithuanian Plaza

My social life
Is finding me asleep on the couch
And therapy sessions,
They often end with a list of things
I forgot to do and mention.
So now I try to explain
Just how I miss the boombox,
Radio Raheem
Do the right thing
And other Spike Lee joints,
I'll get this done by any means necessary.
The battery drains on life
And as I'm trying
To recall the wisdom of an old man
Still living with dreadlocks.
And did I know what was on your mind?
The ether locked in the minds
Will eventually clear
And leave the magnitude of energy.
Now tell me,
How much would you dismiss
A self taught savant?
The Hornets did the same
With 8 and 24,
A decision they will always regret,
Live forever the greatest marksman.
I'm unsure if there was an aptagram
Towards poem
Being lost in the word problem.

Old Edgebrook

I wait as you turn to yourself,
Your shadow extends
Beyond the confines of the floor.
The ghosts of what could have happened
During these sliding doors moments,
Could there be instances
Where you could cross paths and meet?
I don't know how people conjured up
This lackadaisical process to how I think,
Seriously I didn't bother to consider myself
One to talk too much.
Both couldn't be correct.
An American wedding,
But it's not undulating,
That puts the cosmos into perspective.
The universe has good karma today,
The nights breakdown the same
As how Frank switched it.
I'm certain I need a getaway,
What's it like over there?
Is the humidity
Still intent on destroying me?
How can I ever be sure?
So I guess in booking my plane ticket
Isn't so much a crutch,
It's more to pass the time,
Or sense,
Or I don't remember
What the original thought was.
Can anyone tell me if they end up
In a different location from here?

Cabrini-Green

I often try to remember
Words printed on faded off T-shirts
That I donated to people
I can't remember if I remember.
Marcel Duchamp spore art,
For the married woman he was apart
From at the graveyard,
Lipstick remnants
On an unwashed coffee cup,
And the purple swoosh
On the waitresses
Basketball sneakers,
Things hadn't been working for me lately,
That wasn't the synopsis
For these hours.
The words in the soul
Of Bill Withers,
And I'm asked who is he?
Hands cover my mouth
In the shape of a gun,
Removing before the words
Spoke safely.
New words interject,
And all I need is ramen,
What was the name
Of that chess player?
He spoke so vaguely.
The old man didn't answer
My question about ghosts,
How did I not remember that?
The waitress wore her hair
In a blasé,
Though pragmatic fashion.

I guess it was just her way,
Fallback and observe all the words
Between the delays.
Indirect misplace,
Does that oxymoron mean intention?
Pumpkin seeds that became stuck between teeth,
Ceramic heart sprinkled with cinnamon,
As far as premisses went
We had gone through the dysfunction,
And out the other side.
While the kintsugi bowl seemed just so apt,
A rhyme check vibe,
A hundred lost response falling into place
From the gentrification
Which we couldn't avoid.

O'Hare

I didn't feel the need
To inform the world
Of my childhood trauma,
I processed that
In my life that's private.
When asked about my body count,
I asked poets murdered
Or women in bed?
The former's fifteen,
The latter currently stands at seventy-four,
I've not included Amsterdam,
That's simply expensive therapy
For my head.
If I included that
It could have been more.
A reflection on my life
As the bruises shine through
The midnight stars,
What's the final song you want to hear?
Try to describe the bass and guitars,
Did you have plans to speak
In Locrian scale notes?
You know when a sweet dissonance is there,
And all you can do is rewash dull quotes.
The purple will fade outwards to yellow,
It's almost time to fly
Out of O'Hare.
Is Catalan colours a timeless idea retro?
The time on the flight
To reflect on friendships
While playing solitaire.
Directions avoiding the hole in my gut,
The safety starts to runout on my luck.

No.
When all that the room hears
As a retort is what the fuck?

Northalsted Featuring Emily Perkovich

Twenty years in,
This could be considered a midlife crisis,
The gentrification invitation whispers
How this can all be so simple,
Even if it's a drain
On the worlds resources.
Disconnected from this moment
I guess,
This was how I looked after myself
From the trauma.
Vegetarian bagel topped
With grated Gruyère cheese,
I couldn't say even,
The imported taste was priceless.
There were godshots found in everything
If you look or if you please,
Godshots Wanted,
Shout-out to the best book in the city,
Hell, that I ever read.
Didactic choices that fit together.
The tessera pieces forming the mosaic,
Which reminds me of Athena,
The depth reached by a redwood roots,
Maybe the rings of Saturn.
Serenity after the bruises
No longer tessellated out
Of the original pattern.
Functioning through everything,
Paradise wasn't far from here,
Scheol as a wasteland.
I don't regret the mistakes,

This reality and me
don't need a divorce,
We need a break.
Time to navigate through the nadir,
This could be the perfect moment for me
To pass the pen.
Babe, you're romancing these streets,
Rum-soaking, candy-coating,
But I've already sun-dappled the buildings,
Summer-storm-soaked the alleys,
And danced on the rooftops
I'm running out of things to distract me
from saying
There was another shooting last night
Just outside Chicago, 25 miles out, not
Belmont, Boystown, Lakeview
Not quite,
But there's always a casualty at Pride
And that's where my mind slips
Tumbles past the coffee shops and the old
Annoyance Theatre
I can't disconnect it from the trauma
Even though I know the L doesn't even stop
In that neighborhood
Your café slides into the barrel of the gun
Bruises the whole city
Bleeds across the whole city
This city is so fucking bloody
I can't find the godshots.

adam Shove is an Estonian English poet, who writes poems laden with cryptic metaphors and pop culture references; doused in vodka and thrift shop ideas. Inspired by Aesop Rock, Frank Ocean, J Dilla, secondhand clothes, models, tattoos and expensive cars.

RELEASED BY DARK THIRTY POETRY

ANTHOLOGY ONE
THIS ISN'T WHY WE'RE HERE
MORTAL BEINGS
POEMS THAT WERE WRITTEN ON TRAINS BUT
WEREN'T WRITTEN ABOUT TRAINS
CLOSING SHIFT DREAMS
DESIRE
ANIMATE
THESEUS AND I
I DON'T HAVE THE WORDS FOR THIS
CONVERSATIONS BETWEEN THE SUN AND THE
MOON
SLUT POP
JADED
I'VE BIRTHED AN IDEA OF YOU
BRUISES

www.ingramcontent.com/pod-product-compliance
Lightning Source LLC
LaVergne TN
LVHW021455080426
835509LV00018B/2296